I0878536

THE HEART
OF THE
GOOD SHEPHERD
AND THE
HEART OF A PRIEST

The Heart OF THE Good Shepherd AND THE Heart of a Priest

Reflections by
Pope Francis

Edited and with Reflection Questions
by Mark-David Janus, CSP

Paulist Press
New York / Mahwah, NJ

The Scripture quotations contained herein are from the New Revised Standard Version: Catholic Edition, Copyright © 1989 and 1993, by the Division of Christian Education of the National Council of the Churches of Christ in the United States of America. Used by permission. All rights reserved.

Cover and book design by Lynn Else

Copyright © 2016 by Libreria Editrice Vaticana
Introduction and Reflection Questions copyright © 2017 by Paulist Press

All rights reserved. No part of this publication may be reproduced, stored in a retrieval system, or transmitted in any form or by any means, electronic, mechanical, photocopying, recording, scanning, or otherwise, without either the prior written permission of the Publisher, or authorization through payment of the appropriate per-copy fee to the Copyright Clearance Center, Inc., www.copyright.com. Requests to the Publisher for permission should be addressed to the Permissions Department, Paulist Press, permissions@paulistpress.com.

Library of Congress Cataloging-in-Publication Data

Names: Francis, Pope, 1936– author.
Title: The heart of the good shepherd and the heart of a priest : reflections / by Pope Francis.
Description: New York : Paulist Press, 2017.
Identifiers: LCCN 2016054427 | ISBN 9780809153473 (pbk. : alk. paper)
Subjects: LCSH: Meditations.
Classification: LCC BX1378.7 .A25 2017 | DDC 248.4/82—dc23
LC record available at https://lccn.loc.gov/2016054427

ISBN 978-0-8091-5347-3 (paperback)

Published by Paulist Press in 2017
997 Macarthur Boulevard
Mahwah, New Jersey 07430

www.paulistpress.com

Printed and bound in the
United States of America

Contents

Introduction

Pope Francis dedicated several days to praying and talking with his brother priests on the occasion of the Feast of the Sacred Heart of Jesus. These pages capture the Holy Father's intimate thoughts on the love of God, the life of a priest, and the universal call to holiness. His thoughts and prayers are captured in these pages for your reflection.

Perhaps it might be best not to read them all the way through, but rather to begin with a page and read until a specific thought, image, or word strikes you. When it does, stop, put the book down, and invoking the Holy Spirit, spend some time meditating on its meaning in your life and in your service as a priest. Allow this to be your retreat with Pope Francis. These meditations may be useful for private prayer, for your annual retreat, as talking points for your priest support group, or in conversation with your spiritual director.

We have included some reflection questions after each talk, which you may or may not find helpful. What *is* important in this book are the thoughts the Holy Father wanted to share with you, celebrating and supporting your life as a priest.

Fr. Mark-David Janus, CSP, PhD

FIRST MEDITATION

From Estrangement to Celebration

If, as we said, the gospel presents mercy as an excess of God's love, the first thing we have to do is to see where today's world, and every person in it, most needs this kind of overflow of love. We have to ask ourselves how such mercy is to be received. On what barren and parched land must this flood of living water surge? What are the wounds that need this precious balm? What is the sense of abandonment that cries out for loving attention? What is the sense of estrangement that so thirsts for embrace and encounter?

The parable that I would now propose for your meditation is that of the merciful Father (see Luke 15:11–31). We find ourselves before the mystery of the Father. I think we should begin with the moment when the prodigal son stands in the middle of the pigsty, in that inferno of selfishness where, having done everything he wanted to do, now, instead of being free, he feels enslaved. He looks at the pigs as they eat their husks...and he envies them. He feels homesick. He longs for the freshly baked bread that the servants in his house, his father's house, eat for breakfast. Homesickness..., nostalgia. Nostalgia is a powerful emotion. Like mercy, it expands the soul. It makes us think back to our first experience of goodness—the homeland from which we went forth—and it awakens in us the hope of returning there. Against this vast horizon of nostalgia, the young man—as the Gospel tells us—came to his senses and realized that he was miserable.

Without dwelling on that misery of his, let us move on to the other moment, once his father had embraced him and kissed him. He finds himself still dirty, yet dressed for a banquet. He fingers the ring he has been given, which is just like his father's. He has new sandals on his feet. He is in the middle of a party, in the midst of a crowd of people. A bit like ourselves, if ever we have gone to confession before Mass and then all of a sudden found ourselves vested and in the middle of a ceremony.

An Embarrassed Dignity

Let us think for a moment about the "embarrassed dignity" of this prodigal yet beloved son. If we can serenely keep our heart balanced between those two extremes—dignity and embarrassment—without letting go of either of them, perhaps we can feel how the heart of our Father beats with love for us. We can imagine that mercy wells up in it like blood. He goes out to seek us sinners.

He draws us to himself, purifies us, and sends us forth, new and renewed, to every periphery, to bring mercy to all. That blood is the blood of Christ, the blood of the new and eternal covenant of mercy, poured out for us and for all, for the forgiveness of sins. We contemplate that blood by going in and out of his heart and the heart of the Father. That is our sole treasure, the only thing we have to give to the world: the blood that purifies and brings peace to every reality and to all people. The blood of the Lord that forgives sins. The blood that is true drink, for it reawakens and revives what was dead from sin.

In our serene prayer, which wavers between embarrassment and dignity, dignity and embarrassment, let us ask for the grace to sense that mercy as giving meaning to our entire life, the grace to feel how the heart of the Father beats as one with our own. It is not enough to think of that grace as something God offers us from time to time, whenever he forgives some big sin of ours, so that then we can go off to do the rest by ourselves, alone.

Saint Ignatius offers us an image drawn from the courtly culture of his time, but since loyalty among friends is a perennial value, it can also help us. He says that, in order to feel "embarrassment and shame" for our sins (but without forgetting God's mercy), we can use the example of "a knight who finds himself before his king and his entire court, ashamed and embarrassed for having gravely wronged him, after having received from him many gifts and many favors" (*Spiritual Exercises,* 74). But like the prodigal son who finds himself in the middle of a banquet, this knight, who ought to feel ashamed before everyone, suddenly sees the king take him by the hand and restore his dignity. Indeed, not only does the king ask him to follow him into battle, but he puts him at the head of his peers. With what humility and loyalty this knight will serve him henceforth!

Whether we see ourselves as the prodigal son in the midst of the banquet, or the disloyal knight restored and promoted, the important thing is that each of us feels that fruitful tension born of the Lord's mercy: we are at one and the same time sinners pardoned and sinners restored to dignity.

Simon Peter represents the ministerial aspect of this healthy tension. At every step along the way, the Lord trains him to be both Simon and Peter. Simon, the ordinary man with all his faults and inconsistencies, and Peter, the bearer of the keys who leads the others. When Andrew brings Simon, fresh from his nets, to Christ, the Lord gives him the name Peter, "Rock." Yet immediately after praising Peter's confession of faith, which comes from the Father, Jesus sternly reproves him for being tempted to heed the evil spirit telling him to flee the cross. Jesus will go on to invite Peter to walk on the water; he will let him sink into his own fear, only then to stretch out his hand and raise him up. No sooner does Peter confess that he is a sinner than the Lord makes him a fisher of men. He will question Peter at length about his love, instilling in him sorrow and shame for his disloyalty and cowardice, but he will also thrice entrust to him the care of his sheep.

That is how we have to see ourselves: poised between our utter shame and our sublime dignity. Dirty, impure, mean, and selfish, yet at the same time, with feet washed, called and chosen to distribute the Lord's multiplied loaves, blessed by our people, loved and cared for. Only mercy makes this situation bearable. Without it, either we believe in our own righteousness like the Pharisees, or we shrink back like those who feel unworthy. In either case, our hearts grow hardened.

Let us look a little more closely at this and ask why this tension is so fruitful. The reason, I would say, is that it is the result of a free decision. The Lord acts mainly through our freedom, even though his help never fails us. Mercy is a matter of freedom. As a feeling, it wells up spontaneously. When we say that it is visceral, it might seem that it is synonymous with "animal." But animals do not experience "moral" mercy, even though some of them may experience something akin to compassion, like the faithful dog keeping watch at the side of his ailing master. Mercy is a visceral emotion, but it can also be the fruit of an acute intellectual insight—startling as a bolt of lightning but no less complex for its simplicity. We intuit many things when we feel mercy. We understand, for example, that another person is in a desperate state, a limit situation; something is going on that is greater than his or her sins and failings. We also realize that the other person is our peer, that we could well be standing in his or her shoes. Or that evil is such an immense and devastating thing that it can't simply be fixed by justice....Deep down, we realize that what is needed is an infinite mercy, like that of the heart of Christ, to remedy all the evil and suffering we see in the lives of human beings....Anything less than this is not enough. We can understand so many things simply by seeing someone barefoot in the street on a cold morning, or by contemplating the Lord nailed to the cross—for me!

Moreover, mercy can be freely accepted and nurtured, or freely rejected. If we accept it, one thing leads to another. If we choose to ignore it, our heart grows cold. Mercy makes us experience our freedom and, as a result, the freedom of God himself, who, as he said to Moses, is "merciful with whom he is merciful" (cf. Deut 5:10). By his mercy, the Lord expresses his freedom. And we, our own.

We can "do without" the Lord's mercy for a long time. In other words, we can go through life without thinking about it consciously or explicitly asking for it. Then one day we realize that "all is mercy," and we weep bitterly for not having known it earlier, when we needed it most!

This feeling is a kind of moral misery. It is the entirely personal realization that at a certain point in my life I decided to go it alone; I made my choice and I chose badly. Such are the depths we have to reach in order to feel sorrow for our sins and true repentance. Otherwise, we lack the freedom to see that sin affects our entire life. We don't recognize our misery, and thus we miss out on mercy, which only acts on that condition. People don't go to a pharmacy and ask for an aspirin out of mercy. Out of mercy we ask for morphine to administer to a person who is terminally ill and racked with pain.

The heart that God joins to this moral misery of ours is the heart of Christ, his beloved Son, which beats as one with that of the Father and the Spirit. It is a heart that chooses the fastest route and takes it. Mercy gets its hands dirty. It touches, it gets involved, it gets caught up with others, *it gets personal*. It does not approach "cases," but persons and their pain. Mercy exceeds justice; it brings knowledge and compassion; it leads to involvement. By the dignity it brings, mercy raises up the one over whom another has stooped to bring help. The one who shows mercy and the one to whom mercy is shown become equals.

That is why the Father needed to celebrate, so that *everything could be restored at once,* and his son could regain his lost dignity. This realization makes it possible to look to the future in a different way. It is not that mercy overlooks the objective harm brought about by evil. Rather, *it takes away evil's power over the future.* It takes away its power over life, which then goes on. Mercy is the genuine expression of life that counters death, the bitter fruit of sin. As such, it is completely lucid and in no way naïve. It is not that it is blind to evil; rather, it sees how short life is and all the good still to be done. That is why it is so important to forgive completely, so that others can look to the future without wasting time on self-recrimination and self-pity over their past mistakes. In starting to care for others, we will examine our own consciences, and to the extent that we help others, we will make reparation for the wrong we ourselves have done. Mercy is always tinged with hope.

To let ourselves be drawn to and sent by the beating heart of the Father is to remain in this healthy tension of embarrassed dignity. Letting ourselves be drawn into his heart, like blood that has been sullied on its way to give life to the extremities, so that the Lord can purify us and wash our feet. Letting ourselves be sent, full of the oxygen of the Spirit, to revive the whole body, especially those members who are most distant, frail, and hurting.

A priest once told me about a street person who ended up living in a hospice. He was consumed by bitterness and did not interact with others. He was an educated person, as they later found out. Sometime thereafter, this man was hospitalized for a terminal illness. He told the priest that while he was there, feeling empty and disillusioned, the man in the next bed asked him to remove his bedpan and empty it. That request from someone truly in need, someone worse off than he was, opened his eyes and his heart to a powerful sense of humanity, a desire to help another person and to let himself be helped by God. A simple act of mercy put him in touch with infinite mercy. It led him to help someone else and, in doing so, to be helped himself. He died after making a good confession, and at peace.

So I leave you with the parable of the merciful Father, now that we have entered into the situation of the son who feels dirty and dressed up, a dignified sinner, ashamed of himself yet proud of his father. The sign that we have entered into it is that we ourselves now desire to be merciful to all. This is the fire Jesus came to bring to the earth, a fire that lights other fires. If the spark does not take, it is because one of the poles cannot make contact. Either excessive shame, which fails to strip the wires and, instead of freely confessing "I did this or that," stays covered; or excessive dignity, which touches things with gloves.

An Excess of Mercy

The only way for us to be "excessive" in responding to God's excessive mercy is to be completely open to receiving it and sharing it with others. The gospel gives us many touching examples of people who went to excess in order to receive his mercy. There is the paralytic whose friends let him down from the roof into the place where the Lord was preaching. Or the leper who left his nine companions to come back, glorifying and thanking God in a loud voice, to kneel at the Lord's feet. Or the blind Bartimaeus whose outcry made Jesus halt before him. Or the woman suffering from a hemorrhage, who timidly approached the Lord and touched his robe;

as the gospel tells us, Jesus felt power—*dynamis*—"go forth" from him....All of these are examples of that contact that lights a fire and unleashes the positive force of mercy. Then too, we can think of the sinful woman who washed the Lord's feet with her tears and dried them with her hair; Jesus saw her excessive display of love as a sign of her having received great mercy. Ordinary people—sinners, the infirm, and those possessed by demons—are immediately raised up by the Lord. He makes them pass from exclusion to full inclusion, from estrangement to embrace. That is the expression: mercy makes us pass "from estrangement to celebration." And it can only be understood in the key of hope, in an apostolic key, in the key of knowing mercy and then showing mercy.

Let us conclude by praying the Magnificat of mercy, Psalm 51 by King David, which we pray each Friday at Morning Prayer. It is the Magnificat of "a humble and contrite heart," capable of confessing its sin before the God who, in his fidelity, is greater than any of our sins. If we put ourselves in the place of the prodigal son, at the moment when, expecting his Father's reproof, he discovers instead that his Father has thrown a party, we can imagine him praying Psalm 51. We can pray it antiphonally with him. We can hear him saying, "Have mercy on me, O God, in your kindness; in your compassion blot out my offense." And ourselves continuing: "My offenses, truly I (too) know them; my sin is always before me." And together: "Against you, Father, against you, you alone, have I sinned."

May our prayer rise up from that interior tension that kindles mercy, that tension between the shame that says, "From my sins turn away your face, and blot out all my guilt," and the confidence that says, "O purify me, then I shall be clean; O wash me, I shall be whiter than snow." A confidence that becomes apostolic: "Give me again the joy of your help; with the spirit of fervor sustain me, that I may teach transgressors your ways, and sinners may return to you."

PRAYER: Psalm 51

Have mercy on me, O God,
    according to your steadfast love;
according to your abundant mercy
    blot out my transgressions.
Wash me thoroughly from my iniquity,
    and cleanse me from my sin.

For I know my transgressions,
    and my sin is ever before me.
Against you, you alone, have I sinned,
    and done what is evil in your sight,
so that you are justified in your sentence
    and blameless when you pass judgement.
Indeed, I was born guilty,
    a sinner when my mother conceived me.

You desire truth in the inward being;
    therefore teach me wisdom in my secret heart.
Purge me with hyssop, and I shall be clean;
    wash me, and I shall be whiter than snow.
Let me hear joy and gladness;
    let the bones that you have crushed rejoice.
Hide your face from my sins,
    and blot out all my iniquities.

Create in me a clean heart, O God,
    and put a new and right spirit within me.
Do not cast me away from your presence,
    and do not take your holy spirit from me.
Restore to me the joy of your salvation,
    and sustain in me a willing spirit.

Then I will teach transgressors your ways,
    and sinners will return to you.
Deliver me from bloodshed, O God,
    O God of my salvation,
    and my tongue will sing aloud of your deliverance.

O Lord, open my lips,
    and my mouth will declare your praise.
For you have no delight in sacrifice;
    if I were to give a burnt offering, you would not be
        pleased.
The sacrifice acceptable to God is a broken spirit;
    a broken and contrite heart, O God, you will not despise.

Do good to Zion in your good pleasure;
    rebuild the walls of Jerusalem,
then you will delight in right sacrifices,
    in burnt offerings and whole burnt offerings;
    then bulls will be offered on your altar.

Reflection Questions

1. *"Mercy joins a human need to the heart of God, and this leads to immediate action. . . . What are the wounds that need this precious balm? What is the sense of abandonment that cries out for loving attention? What is the sense of estrangement that so thirsts for embrace and encounter?"*

   The Holy Father encourages priests to be ever more ready to receive God's mercy, and encourages us to examine our own needs. Can you identify in your life the wounds, the sense of abandonment, the experience of estrangement that seeks for the embrace and encounter of God? In private prayer or with a spiritual director, can you name them?

2. *"I think we should begin with that moment when the prodigal son stands in the middle of the pigsty, in that inferno of selfishness where having done everything he wanted to do, instead of being free, he feels enslaved. . . . It is the entirely personal realization that at a certain point in my life, I decided to go it alone; I made my choice and I chose badly. We don't recognize our misery, and thus we miss out on mercy, which only acts on that condition."*

   In the course of our priesthood it is easy to "go it alone," to hide from ourselves and others the parts of our humanity that are in need of mercy, healing, and even forgiveness. As priests, we may even feel it is our duty to hide these parts of ourselves from others. We become so skilled at this that we hide not only from ourselves; we hide from God. How do you overcome pride, or shame, and search out God's mercy?

3. *"Letting ourselves be drawn into his heart, like blood that has been sullied on its way to give life to the extremities, so that the Lord can purify us and wash our feet. Letting ourselves be sent, full of the oxygen of the*

Spirit, to revive the whole body, especially those members who are most distant, frail, and hurting."

The Pope encourages priests to let themselves be drawn into the heart of the Father, so that they can be purified with the oxygen of the Spirit. How do you allow yourself to be drawn into the Father's heart? How are you oxygenated with the Holy Spirit?

4. *"We have to speak of what moves us, of those faces that make us want to do something to satisfy their hunger and thirst for God, for justice, for tenderness. . . .Mercy gets its hands dirty. It touches, it gets involved, it gets caught up with others."*

   Close your eyes and think of the people to whom you minister. Whose faces move you? What do you see in them that compels you to become involved as an agent of the works of mercy on their behalf?

SECOND MEDITATION

The Vessel of Mercy

The vessel of mercy is our sin. Our sin is usually like a sieve, or a leaky bucket, from which grace quickly drains. "For my people have committed two evils: they have forsaken me, the fountain of living water, and dug out cisterns for themselves, cracked cisterns that can hold no water" (Jer 2:13). That is why the Lord had to teach Peter the need to "forgive seventy times seven." God keeps forgiving, even though he sees how hard it is for his grace to take root in the parched and rocky soil of our hearts. He never stops sowing his mercy and his forgiveness.

Hearts Created Anew

Let us take a closer look at this mercy of God that is always "greater" than our consciousness of our sinfulness. The Lord never tires of forgiving us; indeed, he renews the wineskins in which we receive that forgiveness. He uses a new wineskin for the new wine of his mercy, not one that is patched or old. That wineskin is mercy itself: his own mercy, which we experience and then show in helping others. A heart that has known mercy is not old and patched, but new and re-created. It is the heart for which David prayed: "A pure heart create for me, O God, put a steadfast spirit within me" (Ps 51:10).

That heart, created anew, is a good vessel; it is no longer battered and leaky. The liturgy echoes the heartfelt conviction of the Church in the beautiful prayer that follows the first reading of the Easter Vigil: "O God who wonderfully created the universe, then more wonderfully re-created it in the redemption." In this prayer, we affirm that the second creation is even more wondrous than the first. Ours is a heart conscious of having been created anew thanks to the coalescence of its own poverty and God's forgiveness; it is a "heart which has been shown mercy and shows mercy." It feels the balm of grace poured out upon its wounds and its sinfulness; it feels mercy assuaging its guilt, watering its aridity with love and rekindling its hope. When, with the same grace, it then forgives other sinners and treats them with compassion, this mercy takes root in good soil, where water does not drain off, but sinks in and gives life.

The best practitioners of this mercy that rights wrongs are those who know that they themselves are forgiven and sent to help others. We see this with addiction counselors: those who have overcome their own addiction are usually those who can best understand, help, and challenge others. So too, the best confessors are usually themselves good penitents. Almost all the great saints were great sinners or, like Saint Therese, knew that it was by sheer grace that they were not.

The real vessel of mercy, then, is *the mercy that each of us received and that created in us a new heart.* This is the "new wineskin" to which Jesus referred (cf. Luke 5:37), the "healed sore."

Here we enter more deeply into the mystery of the Son, Jesus, who is the Father's mercy incarnate. Here, too, we can find the definitive icon of the vessel of mercy in the wounds of the risen Lord. Those wounds remind us that the traces of our sins, forgiven by God, never completely heal or disappear; they remain as scars. Scars are sensitive; they do not hurt, yet they remind us of our old wounds. God's mercy is in those scars. In the scars of the risen Christ, the marks of the wounds in his hands and feet but also in his pierced heart, we find the true meaning of sin and grace. As we contemplate the wounded heart of the Lord, we see ourselves reflected in him. His heart and our own are similar; both are wounded and risen. But we know that his heart was pure love and was wounded because it willed to be so; our heart, on the other hand, was pure wound, which was healed because it allowed itself to be loved.

Our Saints Received Mercy

We can benefit from contemplating others who let their hearts be re-created by mercy and by seeing the "vessel" in which they received that mercy. *Paul* received mercy in the harsh and inflexible vessel of his judgment, shaped by the Law. His harsh judgment made him a persecutor. Mercy so changed him that he sought those who were far off, from the pagan world, and at the same time, showed great understanding and mercy to those who were as he had been. Paul was willing to be an outcast, provided he could save his own people. His approach can be summed up in this way: he did not judge even himself, but instead let himself be justified by a God who is greater than his conscience, appealing to Jesus as the faithful advocate from whose love nothing and no one could separate him. Paul's understanding of God's unconditional mercy was radical. His realization that God's mercy overcomes the inner wound that subjects us to two laws, the law of the flesh and the law of the Spirit, was the fruit of a mind open to absolute truth, wounded in the very place where the Law and the Light become a trap. The famous "thorn" that the Lord did not take away from him was the vessel in which Paul received the Lord's mercy (cf. 2 Cor 12:7).

Peter receives mercy in his presumption of being a man of good sense. He was sensible with the sound, practical wisdom of a fisherman who knows from experience when to fish and when not to. But he was also sensible when, in his excitement at walking on water and hauling in miraculous draughts of fish, he gets carried away with himself and realizes that he has to ask help from the only one who can save him. Peter was healed of the deepest wound of all, that of denying his friend. Perhaps the reproach of Paul, who confronted him with his duplicity, has to do with this; it may be that Paul felt that he had been worse "before" knowing Christ, whereas Peter had denied Christ, after knowing him. Still, once Peter was healed of that wound, he became a merciful pastor, a solid rock on which one can always build, since it is a weak rock that has been healed, not a stumbling stone. In the Gospel, Peter is the disciple whom the Lord most often corrects. Jesus is constantly correcting him, even to the end: "What is that to you? Follow me!" (John 21:22). Tradition tells us that Jesus appeared once again to Peter as he was fleeing Rome. The image of Peter being crucified head down perhaps best expresses this vessel of a hardhead who, in order to be shown mercy, abased himself even in giving the supreme witness of his love for the Lord. Peter did not want to end his life saying, "I learned the lesson," but rather, "Since my head is never going to get it right, I will put it on the bottom." What he put on top were his feet, the feet that the Lord had washed. For Peter, those feet were the vessel in which he received the mercy of his Friend and Lord.

John was healed in his pride for wanting to requite evil with fire. He who was a "Son of Thunder" (Mark 3:17) would end up writing to his "little children" and would seem like a kindly grandfather who speaks only of love.

Augustine was healed in his regret for being a latecomer: "Late have I loved thee." He would find a creative and loving way to make up for lost time by writing his *Confessions.*

Francis experienced mercy at many points in his life. Perhaps the definitive vessel, which became real wounds, was not so much kissing the leper, marrying Lady Poverty, or feeling himself a brother to every creature, as the experience of having to watch over in merciful silence the order he had founded. Francis saw his brethren divided under the very banner of poverty. The devil makes us quarrel among ourselves, defending even the most holy things "with an evil spirit."

Ignatius was healed in his vanity, and if that was the vessel, we can catch a glimpse of how great his yearning for vainglory must have been, which was re-created in his strenuous efforts to seek the greater glory of God.

In his *Diary of a Country Priest* (Da Capo Press, 2002), Georges Bernanos recounts the life of an ordinary priest, inspired by the life of the Curé of Ars. There are two beautiful paragraphs describing the reflections of the priest in the final moments of his unexpected illness: "May God grant me the grace in these last weeks to continue to take care of the parish....But I shall give less thought to the future, I shall work in the present. I feel such work is within my power. For I only succeed in small things, and when I am tried by anxiety, I am bound to say that it is the small things that release me." Here we see a small vessel of mercy, one that has to do with the minuscule joys of our pastoral life, where we receive and bestow the infinite mercy of the Father in little gestures.

The other paragraph says, "It is all over now. The strange mistrust I had of myself, of my own being, has flown, I believe forever. That conflict is done. I cannot understand it any more. I am reconciled to myself, to the poor, poor shell of me. How easy it is to hate oneself. True grace is to forget. Yet if pride could die in us, the supreme grace would be to love oneself in all simplicity—as one would love any of those who themselves have suffered and loved in Christ." This is the vessel: "to love oneself in all simplicity, as one would love any of those who themselves have suffered and loved in Christ." It is an ordinary vessel, like an old jar we can borrow even from the poor.

Blessed José Gabriel del Rosario Brochero, the Argentinian priest soon to be canonized, "let his heart be shaped by the mercy of God." In the end, his vessel was his own leprous body. He wanted to die on horseback, crossing a mountain stream on the way to anoint a sick person. Among the last things he said was, "There is no ultimate glory in this life"; "I am quite happy with what God has done with me regarding my sight, and I thank him for that. While I could serve other people, he kept my senses whole and strong. Today, when I can no longer do so, he has taken away one of my physical senses. In this world there is no ultimate glory, and we have our more than enough misery." Often our work remains unfinished, so being at peace with that is always a grace. We are allowed to "let things go," so that the Lord can bless and perfect them. We shouldn't be overly concerned. In this way, we can be open to the pain and joy of our brothers and sisters.

Cardinal *Van Thuan* used to say that, in prison, the Lord taught him to distinguish between "God's business," to which he was devoted in his free life as priest and bishop, and God himself, to whom he was devoted during his imprisonment (*Five Loaves and Two Fish,* Pauline Books and Media, 2003).

Mary as a Vessel and Source of Mercy

Ascending the stairway of the saints in our pursuit of vessels of mercy, we come at last to Our Lady. She is the simple yet perfect vessel who both receives and bestows mercy. Her free "yes" to grace is the very opposite of the sin that led to the downfall of the prodigal son. Her mercy is very much her own, very much our own, and very much that of the Church. As she says in the Magnificat, she knows that God has looked with favor upon her humility, and she recognizes that his mercy is from generation to generation. Mary can see the working of this mercy and she feels "embraced," together with all of Israel, by it. She treasures in her heart the memory and promise of God's infinite mercy for his people. Hers is the Magnificat of a pure and overflowing heart that sees all of history and each individual person with a mother's mercy.

During the moments I was able to spend alone with Mary during my visit to Mexico, as I gazed at Our Lady, the Virgin of Guadalupe and I let her gaze at me, I prayed for you, dear priests, to be good pastors of souls. In my address to the bishops, I mentioned that I have often reflected on the mystery of Mary's gaze, its tenderness and its sweetness that give us the courage to open our hearts to God's mercy. I would now like to reflect with you on a few of the ways that Our Lady "gazes" especially at priests, since through us she wants to gaze at her people.

Mary's gaze makes us feel her maternal embrace. She shows us that "the only power capable of winning human hearts is the tenderness of God. What delights and attracts, humbles and overcomes, opens and unleashes is not the power of instruments or the force of the law, but rather the omnipotent weakness of divine love, which is the irresistible force of its gentleness and the irrevocable pledge of its mercy" (*Address to the Mexican Bishops,* February 13, 2016). What people seek in the eyes of Mary is "a place of rest where people, still orphans and disinherited, may find a place of refuge, a home." And that has to do with the way she "gazes"—her eyes open up a space that is inviting, not at all like a tribunal or an office. If, at times, people realize that their own gaze has become hardened, that they tend to look at people with annoyance or coldness, they can turn back to her in heartfelt humility. For Our Lady can remove every "cataract" that prevents them from seeing Christ in people's souls. She can remove the myopia that fails to see the needs of others, which are the needs of the incarnate Lord, as well as the hyperopia that cannot see the details, "the small print," where the truly important things are played out in the life of the Church and of the family.

Another aspect of Mary's gaze has to do with weaving. Mary gazes "by weaving," by finding a way to bring good out of all the things that her people lay at her feet. I told the Mexican bishops that "in the mantle of the Mexican soul, with the thread of its *mestizo* features, God has woven in *la Morenita* the face by which he wishes to be known." A spiritual master teaches us that "whatever is said of Mary specially is said of the Church universally and of each soul individually" (cf. Isaac of Stella, *Serm.* 51: PL 194, 1863). If we consider how God wove the face and figure of Our Lady of Guadalupe into Juan Diego's cloak, we can prayerfully ponder how he is weaving our soul and the life of the whole Church.

They say that it is impossible to see how the image of Our Lady of Guadalupe was "painted"; it seems to have been somehow "imprinted." I like to think that the miracle was not only that the image was imprinted or painted, but that the entire cloak was re-created, transformed from top to bottom. Each thread—those threads of maguey leaf that women had learned from childhood to weave for their finest garments—was transfigured in its place and, interwoven with all the others, revealed the face of our Lady, her presence, and her surroundings. God's mercy does the same thing. It doesn't "paint" us a pretty face or airbrush the reality of who we are. Rather, with the very threads of our poverty and sinfulness, interwoven with the Father's love, it so weaves us that our soul is renewed and recovers its true image, the image of Jesus. So be priests "capable of imitating this freedom of God, who chooses the humble in order to reveal the majesty of his countenance, priests capable of imitating God's patience by weaving the new humanity which your country awaits with the fine thread of all those whom you encounter. Don't give into the temptation to go elsewhere, as if the love of God were not powerful enough to bring about change" (*Address to the Mexican Bishops,* February 13, 2016).

A third aspect is that of attentive care. Mary's gaze is one of complete attention. She leaves everything else behind, and is concerned only with the person in front of her. Like a mother, she is all ears for the child who has something to tell her. "As the wonderful Guadalupe tradition teaches us, *la Morenita* treasures the gaze of all those who look to her; she reflects the faces of all who come to her. There is something unique in the face of every person who comes to us looking for God. We need to realize this, to open our hearts, and to show concern for them. Only a Church capable of attentive concern for all those who knock on her door can speak to them of God. Unless we can see into people's suffering and recognize their needs, we will have nothing to offer them. The riches we possess only flow forth when we truly encounter the needs of others, and this encounter take places precisely in our heart as pastors" (ibid.). I asked your bishops to be attentive to you, their priests, and not to leave you "exposed to loneliness and abandonment, easy prey to a worldliness that devours the heart" (ibid.). The world is watching us closely, in order to "devour" us, to make us consumers....All of us need attention, a gaze of genuine concern. As I told the bishops: "Be attentive and learn to read the faces of your priests, in order to rejoice with them when they feel the joy of recounting all that they have 'done and taught' (*Mk* 6:30). Also do not step back when they are humbled and can only weep because they 'have denied the Lord' (cf. *Lk* 22:61–62). Offer your support, in communion with Christ, whenever one of them, discouraged, goes out with Judas into 'the night' (cf. *Jn* 13:30). In these situations your fatherly care for your priests must never be found wanting. Encourage communion among them; seek to bring out the best in them, and enlist them in great ventures, for the heart of an apostle was not made for small things" (ibid.).

Last, Mary's gaze is "integral," all-embracing. It brings everything together: our past, our present, and our future. It is not fragmented or partial: *mercy can see things as a whole and grasp what is most necessary*. At Cana, Mary "empathetically" foresaw what the lack of wine in the wedding feast would mean, and she asked Jesus to resolve the problem, without anyone noticing. We can see our entire priestly life as somehow "foreseen" by Mary's mercy; she sees beforehand the things we lack and provides for them. If there is any "good wine" present in our lives, it is due not to our own merits but to her "anticipated mercy." In the Magnificat, she proclaims how the Lord "looked with favor on her loneliness" and "remembered his (covenant of) mercy," a "mercy shown from generation to generation" to the poor and the downtrodden. For Mary, history is mercy.

We can conclude by praying the Salve Regina. The words of this prayer are vibrant with the mystery of the Magnificat. Mary is the Mother of mercy, our life, our sweetness, and our hope. Her eyes of mercy are surely the greatest vessel of mercy, for their gaze enables us to drink in that kindness and goodness for which we hunger with a yearning that a look of love alone can satisfy. Her eyes of mercy also enable us to see God's mercy at work in human history and to find Jesus in the faces of our brothers and sisters. In Mary, we catch a glimpse of the promised land—the kingdom of mercy established by our Lord—already present in this life beyond the exile into which sin leads us. From her hand and beneath her gaze, we can joyfully proclaim the greatness of the Lord. To Mary we can say, My soul sings of you, Lord, for you have looked with favor on the lowliness and humility of your servant. How blessed I am to have been forgiven. Your mercy, Lord, that you showed to your saints and to all your faithful people, you have also shown to me. I was lost, seeking only myself, in the arrogance of my heart, yet I found no glory. My only glory is that your Mother has embraced me, covered me with her mantle, and drawn me to her heart. I want to be loved as one of your little ones. I want to feed with your bread all those who hunger for you. Remember, Lord, your covenant of mercy with your sons, the priests of your people. With Mary, may we be the sign and sacrament of your mercy.

PRAYER: The Magnificat (NRSV)

My soul magnifies the Lord,
and my spirit rejoices in God my Savior,
for he has looked with favor on the lowliness of his servant.
Surely, from now on all generations will call me blessed;
for the Mighty One has done great things for me,
and holy is his name.
His mercy is for those who fear him
from generation to generation.
He has shown strength with his arm;
he has scattered the proud in the thoughts of their hearts.
He has brought down the powerful from their thrones,
and lifted up the lowly;

he has filled the hungry with good things,
and sent the rich away empty.
He has helped his servant Israel,
in remembrance of his mercy,
according to the promise he made to our ancestors,
to Abraham and to his descendants forever.

Reflection Questions

1. *"Here, too, we can find the definitive icon of the vessel of mercy in the wounds of the risen Lord. Those wounds remind us that the traces of our sins, forgiven by God, never completely heal or disappear; they remain as scars. Scars are sensitive; they do not hurt, yet they remind us of our old wounds. God's mercy is in those scars."*

   In which of your scars does God's mercy reside? What do your scars teach you about yourself? About God?
2. *"As we contemplate the wounded heart of the Lord, we see ourselves reflected in him. His heart, and our own, are similar: both are wounded and risen. But we know that his heart was pure love and was wounded because it willed to be so; our heart, on the other hand, was pure wound, which was healed because it allowed itself to be loved."*

   Pope Francis speaks of our heart as wounded and risen, healed because it allowed itself to be loved. In what ways is your heart loved? In what ways does your heart not allow itself to be loved?
3. *"Peter was healed of the deepest wound of all, that of denying his friend."*

   The Holy Father speaks of being healed of the deepest wound of all—for you. What is your deepest wound?

Have you allowed it to be healed as Peter allowed Jesus to heal him? Is your own healing ongoing? Does your own story embarrass you or inspire you?

4. *"What people seek in the eyes of Mary is 'a place of rest where people, still orphans and disinherited, may find a place of refuge, a home.'. . .If, at times, people realize that their own gaze has become hardened, that they tend to look at people with annoyance or coldness, they can turn back to her in heartfelt humility. For Our Lady can remove every 'cataract' that prevents them from seeing Christ in people's souls."*

   With what eyes do you look at the people of God? What "cataracts" unique to you prevent you from seeing Christ in their souls?

5. *"Only a Church capable of attentive concern for all those who knock on her door can speak to them of God. Unless we can see into people's suffering and recognize their needs, we will have nothing to offer them. The riches we possess only flow forth when we truly encounter the needs of others, and this encounter take places precisely in our heart as pastors."*

   In your ministry, what competes for your attention? What factors make it difficult for you to pay attention to the people who come to you?

6. *"If we consider how God wove the face and figure of Our Lady of Guadalupe into Juan Diego's cloak, we can prayerfully ponder how he is weaving our soul and the life of the whole Church."*

   The Holy Father uses the metaphor of weaving—God weaving us into the life of the Church. Throughout your priesthood, have you experienced your life being woven into the life of the people of God? What has that process been like for you?

THIRD MEDITATION

The Good Odor of Christ and the Light of His Mercy

In this, our third meeting, I propose that we meditate on the works of mercy, by taking whichever one we feel is most closely linked to our charism, and by looking at them as a whole. We can contemplate them through the merciful eyes of Our Lady, who helps us to find "the wine that is lacking" and encourages us to "do whatever Jesus tells us" (cf. John 2:1–12), so that his mercy can work the miracles that our people need.

The works of mercy are closely linked to the "spiritual senses." In our prayer, we ask for the grace to "feel and savor" the gospel, that it can make us more "sensitive" in our lives. Moved by the Spirit and led by Jesus, we can see from afar, with the eyes of mercy, those who have fallen along the wayside. We can hear the cries of Bartimaeus, and feel with Jesus the timid yet determined touch of the woman suffering from hemorrhage, as she grasps his robe. We can ask for the grace to taste, with the crucified Jesus, the bitter gall of all those who share in his cross, and smell the stench of misery—in field hospitals, in trains, and in boats crammed with people. The balm of mercy does not disguise this stench. Rather, by anointing it, it awakens new hope.

The *Catechism of the Catholic Church,* in discussing the works of mercy, tells us that "when her mother reproached her for care for the poor and the sick at home, Saint Rose of Lima said to her: 'When we serve the poor and the sick, we are the good odor of Christ'" (no. 2449, Latin). That good odor of Christ—the care of the poor—is, and always has been, the hallmark of the Church. Paul made it the focus of his meeting with Peter, James, and John, the "columns" of the Church. He tells us that they "asked only one thing, that we remember the poor" (Gal 2:10). The *Catechism* goes on to say, significantly, that "those who are oppressed by poverty are the object of *a preferential love* on the part of the Church, which from her origins, and in spite of the failings of many of her members, has not ceased to work for their relief, defense and liberation" (no. 2448).

In the Church we have, and have always had, our sins and failings. But when it comes to serving the poor by the works of mercy, as a Church we have always followed the promptings of the Spirit. Our saints did this in quite creative and effective ways. Love for the poor has been the sign, the light that draws people to give glory to the Father. Our people value this in a priest who cares for the poor and the sick, for those whose sins he forgives and for those whom he patiently teaches and corrects….Our people forgive us priests many failings, except for that of attachment to money. This does not have so much to do with money itself, but the fact that money makes us lose the treasure of mercy. Our people can sniff out which sins are truly grave for a priest, the sins that kill his ministry because they turn him into a bureaucrat or, even worse, a mercenary. They can also recognize which sins are, I won't say secondary, but that have to be put up with, borne like a cross, until the Lord at last burns them away like the chaff. But the failure of a priest to be merciful is a glaring contradiction. It strikes at the heart of salvation, against Christ, who "became poor so that by his poverty we might become rich" (cf. 2 Cor 8:9), because mercy heals "by losing something of itself." We feel a pang of regret and we lose a part of our life, because rather than do what we wanted to do, we reached out to someone else.

So it is not about God showing me mercy for this or that sin, as if I were otherwise self-sufficient, or about us performing some act of mercy toward this or that person in need. The grace we seek in this prayer is that of letting ourselves be shown mercy by God in *every* aspect of our lives and, in turn, to show mercy to others in all that we do. As priests and bishops, we work with the sacraments, baptizing, hearing confessions, celebrating the Eucharist. . . .Mercy is our way of making the entire life of God's people a sacrament. Being merciful is not only "a way of life," but "*the* way of life." There is no other way of being a priest. Father Brochero, soon to be canonized, put it this way: "The priest who has scarce pity for sinners is only half a priest. These vestments I wear are not what make me a priest; if I don't have charity in my heart, I am not even a Christian."

To see needs and to bring immediate relief, and even more, to anticipate those needs: this is the mark of a father's gaze. This priestly gaze, which takes the place of the father in the heart of Mother Church, makes us see people with the eyes of mercy. It has to be learned from seminary on, and it must enrich all our pastoral plans and projects. We desire, and we ask the Lord to give us, a gaze capable of discerning the signs of the times, to know "what works of mercy our people need today" in order to feel and savor the God of history who walks among them. For, as Aparecida says, quoting Saint Alberto Hurtado, "In our works, our people know that we understand their suffering" (no. 386). In our works…

The proof that we understand is that our works of mercy are blessed by God and are met with help and cooperation from our people. Some plans and projects do not work out well, without people ever realizing why. They rack their brains trying to come up with yet another pastoral plan, when all somebody has to say is, "It's not working because it lacks mercy," with no further ado. If it is not blessed, it is because it lacks mercy. It lacks the mercy found in a field hospital, not in expensive clinics; it lacks the mercy that values goodness and opens the door to an encounter with God, rather than turning someone away with sharp criticism…

I am going to propose a prayer about the woman whose sins were forgiven (John 8:3–11), to ask for the grace to be merciful in the confessional, and another prayer about the social dimension of the works of mercy.

I have always been struck by the passage of the Lord's encounter with the woman caught in adultery, and how, by refusing to condemn her, he "fell short of" the law. In response to the question they asked to test him—"should she be stoned or not?"—he did not rule, he did not apply the law. He played dumb, and then turned to something else. He thus initiated a process in the heart of the woman who needed to hear those words: "Neither do I condemn you." He stretched out his hand and helped her to her feet, letting her see a gentle gaze that changed her heart.

Sometimes I feel a little saddened and annoyed when people go straight to the last words Jesus speaks to her: "Go and sin no more." They use these words to "defend" Jesus from bypassing the law. I believe that Christ's words are of a piece with his actions. He bends down to write on the ground as a prelude to what he is about to say to those who want to stone the woman, and he does so again before talking to her. This tells us something about the "time" that the Lord takes in judging and forgiving, the time he gives each person to look into his or her own heart and then to walk away. In talking to the woman, the Lord opens other spaces: one is that of noncondemnation. The gospel clearly mentions this open space. It makes us see things through the eyes of Jesus, who tells us, "I see no one else but this woman."

Then Jesus makes the woman herself look around. He asks her, "Where are those who condemned you?" (The word *condemn* is itself important, since it is about what we find unacceptable about those who judge or caricature us.) Once he has opened before her eyes this space freed of other people's judgments, he tells her that neither will he throw a stone there: "Nor do I condemn you." Then he opens up another free space before her: "Go and sin no more." His command has to do with the future, to help her to make a new start and to "walk in love." Such is the sensitivity of mercy: it looks with compassion on the past and offers encouragement for the future.

Those words, "Go and sin no more," are not easy. The Lord says them "with her." He helps her put into words what she herself feels, a free "no" to sin that is like Mary's "yes" to grace. That "no" has to be said to the deeply rooted sin present in everyone. In that woman, it was a social sin; people approached her either to sleep with her or to throw stones at her. That is why the Lord does not only clear the path before her, but sets her on her way, so that she can stop being the "object" of other people's gaze and instead take control of her life. Those words, "sin no more," refer not only to morality, but, I believe, to a kind of sin that keeps her from living her life. Jesus also told the paralytic at Bethzatha to sin no more (John 5:14). But that man had justified himself with all the sad things that had "happened to him"; he suffered from a victim complex. So Jesus challenged him ever so slightly by saying, "lest something worse happen to you." The Lord took advantage of his way of thinking, his fears, to draw him out of his paralysis. He gave him a little scare, we might say. The point is that each of us has to hear the words "sin no more" in his own deeply personal way.

This image of the Lord who sets people on their way is very typical. He is the God who walks at his people's side, who leads them forward, who accompanies our history. Hence, the object of his mercy is quite clear: it is everything that keeps a man or a woman from walking on the right path, with their own people, at their own pace, to where God is asking them to go. What troubles him is that people get lost, or fall behind, or try to go it on their own, that they end up nowhere. That they are not there for the Lord, ready to go wherever he wants to send them. That they do not walk humbly before him (cf. Mic 6:8), that they do not walk in love (cf. Eph 5:2).

The Space of the Confessional, Where the Truth Makes Us Free

Speaking of space, let us go to the confessional. The *Catechism of the Catholic Church* presents the confessional as the place where the truth makes us free for an encounter. "When he celebrates the sacrament of penance, the priest is fulfilling the ministry of the Good Shepherd who seeks the lost sheep, of the Good Samaritan who binds up wounds, of the Father who awaits the prodigal son and welcomes him on his return, and of the just and impartial Judge whose judgment is both just and merciful. The priest is the sign and the instrument of God's merciful love for the sinner" (no. 1465). The Catechism also reminds us that "the confessor is not the master of God's forgiveness but its servant. The minister of this sacrament should unite himself to the intention and charity of Christ" (no. 1466).

Signs and instruments of an encounter; that is what we are: an attractive invitation to an encounter. As signs, we must be welcoming, sending a message that attracts people's attention. Signs need to be consistent and clear, but above all, understandable. Some signs are only clear to specialists. Signs and instruments. Instruments have to be effective, readily available, precise, and suitable for the job. We are instruments if people have a genuine encounter with the God of mercy. Our task is "to make that encounter possible," face-to-face. What people do afterward is their business. There is a prodigal son among the pigs and a father who goes out every afternoon to see if he is returning. There is a lost sheep and a shepherd who goes out to seek him. There is a wounded person left at the roadside and a good-hearted Samaritan. What is our ministry? It is to be signs and instruments enabling this encounter. Let us always remember that we are not the father, the shepherd, or the Samaritan. Rather, inasmuch as we are sinners, we are on the side of the other three. Our ministry has to be a sign and instrument of that encounter. We are part of the mystery of the Holy Spirit, who creates the Church, builds unity, and constantly invites to encounter.

The other mark of a sign and instrument is that *it is not self-referential*. Put more simply, it is not an end in itself. Nobody sticks with the sign once they understand the reality. Nobody keeps looking at the screwdriver or the hammer, but at the well-hung picture. We are useless servants; instruments and signs that help two people to join in an embrace, like the father and his son.

The third mark of a sign and instrument is its *availability*. An instrument has to be readily accessible; a sign must be visible. Being a sign and instrument is about being a *mediator*. Perhaps this is the real key to our own mission in this merciful encounter of God and man. We could even put it in negative terms. Saint Ignatius talked about "not getting in the way." A good mediator makes things easy, rather than setting up obstacles. In my country, there was a great confessor, Father Cullen. He would sit in the confessional and do one of two things: he would repair worn soccer balls for the local kids, or he would thumb through a big Chinese dictionary. He used to say that when people saw him doing such completely useless things like fixing old soccer balls or trying to master Chinese, they would think, "I'm going to go up and talk to this priest, since he obviously doesn't have much to do!" He was available for what was essential. He got rid of the obstacle of always looking busy and serious.

Everybody has known good confessors. We have to learn from our good confessors, the ones whom people seek out, who do not make them afraid but help them to speak frankly, as Jesus did with Nicodemus. If people come to confession, it is because they are penitent; *repentance* is already present. They come to confession because they want to change, or at least they want to want to change if they think their situation is impossible. *Ad impossibilia nemo tenetur,* as the old maxim goes: no one is obliged to do the impossible.

We have to learn from good confessors, those who are gentle with sinners, who after a couple of words understand everything, as Jesus did with the woman suffering from a hemorrhage, and straightaway the power of forgiveness goes forth from them. The *integrity* of confession is not a mathematics problem. Sometimes people feel less shame in confessing a sin than in stating the number of times they committed it. We have to let ourselves be moved by people's situations, which at times is a mixture of their own doing, human weakness, sin, and insuperable conditionings. We have to be like Jesus, who was deeply moved by the sight of people and their problems, and kept healing them, even when they "didn't ask properly," like that leper, or seemed to beat around the bush, like the Samaritan woman. She was like a bird we have in South America: she squawked in one place but had her nest in another.

We have to learn from confessors who can enable penitents to feel *amendment* in taking a small step forward, like Jesus, who gave a suitable penance and could appreciate the one leper who returned to thank him, on whom he bestowed yet more. Jesus had his mat taken away from the paralytic, and he made the blind man and the Syro-Phoenician woman have to ask. It didn't matter to him if they paid no attention to him, like the paralytic at the pool of

Bethzatha, or told others what he ordered them not to tell, with the result that he himself became the leper, since he could not go into the towns or his enemies found reasons to condemn him. He healed people, forgave their sins, eased their suffering, gave them rest, and made them feel the consoling breath of the Spirit.

In Buenos Aires, I knew a Capuchin Friar. He is a little younger than myself and a great confessor. There is always a line before his confessional, lots of people confessing all day long. He is really good at forgiving. He forgives, but every once in a while he has scruples about being so forgiving. Once in conversation he told me, "Sometimes I have scruples." So I asked him, "What do you do when you have these scruples?" He replied, "I go before the tabernacle, I look at our Lord and I tell him, 'Lord, forgive me, today I was very forgiving. But let's be clear, it is all your fault, because you gave me bad example!'" He added mercy to mercy.

Last, as far as confession is concerned, I have two bits of advice. First, never look like a bureaucrat or a judge, somebody who just sees "cases" to be dealt with. Mercy sets us free from being this kind of priest, who is so used to judging "cases" that he is no longer sensitive to persons, to faces. The rule of Jesus is to "judge as we would be judged." This is the key to our judgment: that we treat others with dignity, that we don't demean or mistreat them, that we help raise them up, and that we never forget that the Lord is using us, weak as we are, as his instruments—not necessarily because our judgment is "the best," but because it is sincere and can build a good relationship.

My other bit of advice is not to be curious in the confessional. Saint Therese tells us that when her novices would confide in her, she was very careful not to ask how things turned out. She did not pry into people's souls (cf. *The Story of a Soul,* Manuscript C, to Mother Gonzaga, c. XII, 32r.). It is characteristic of mercy to cover sin with its cloak, so as not to wound people's dignity; like the two sons of Noah, who covered with a cloak the nakedness of their father in his drunkenness (cf. Gen 9:23).

The Social Dimension of the Works of Mercy

At the end of the Exercises, Saint Ignatius puts "contemplation to attain love," which connects what is experienced in prayer to daily life. He makes us reflect on how love has to be put more into works than into words. Those works are the works of mercy that the Father "prepared beforehand to be our way of life" (Eph 2:10), those that the Spirit inspires in each for the common good (cf. 1 Cor 12:7). In thanking the Lord for all the gifts we have received from his bounty, we ask for the grace to bring to all mankind that mercy that has been our own salvation.

I propose that we meditate on one of the final paragraphs of the Gospels. There, the Lord himself makes that connection between what we have received and what we are called to give. We can read these conclusions in the key of "works of mercy," which bring about the time of the Church, the time in which the risen Jesus lives, guides, sends forth, and appeals to our freedom, which finds in him its concrete daily realization.

Matthew tells us that the Lord sends his apostles to make disciples of all nations, "teaching them to obey everything that I have commanded" (28:20). This "instructing the ignorant" is itself one of the works of mercy. It spreads like light to the other works: to those listed in Matthew 25, which deal more with the so-called corporal works of mercy, and to all the commandments and evangelical counsels, such as forgiving, fraternally correcting, consoling the sorrowing, and enduring persecution....

Mark's Gospel ends with the image of the Lord who "collaborates" with the apostles and "confirms the word by the signs that accompany it." Those "signs" greatly resemble the works of mercy. Mark speaks, among other things, of healing the sick and casting out demons (cf. 16:17–18).

Luke continues his Gospel with the "Acts"—*praxeis*—of the apostles, relating the history of how they acted and the works they did, led by the Spirit.

John's Gospel ends by referring to the "many other things" (21:25) or "signs" (20:30) that Jesus performed. The Lord's actions, his works, are not mere deeds but signs by which, in a completely personal way, he shows his love and his mercy for each person.

We can contemplate the Lord who sends us on this mission, by using the image of the merciful Jesus as revealed to Sister Faustina. In that image we can see mercy as a single ray of light that comes from deep within God, passes through the heart of Christ, and emerges in a diversity of colors, each representing a work of mercy.

The works of mercy are endless, but each bears the stamp of a particular face, a personal history. They are much more than the lists of the seven corporal and seven spiritual works of mercy. Those lists are like the raw material—the material of life itself—that, worked and shaped by the hands of mercy, turns into an individual artistic creation. Each work multiplies like the bread in the baskets; each gives abundant growth like the mustard seed. For mercy is fruitful and inclusive.

We usually think of the works of mercy individually and in relation to a specific initiative: hospitals for the sick, soup kitchens for the hungry, shelters for the homeless, schools for those to be educated, the confessional and spiritual direction for those needing counsel and forgiveness….But if we look at the works of mercy as a whole, we see that the object of mercy is human life itself and everything it embraces. Life itself, as "flesh," hungers and thirsts; it needs to be clothed, given shelter, and visited, to say nothing of receiving a proper burial, something none of us, however rich, can do for ourselves. Even the wealthiest person, in death, becomes a pauper; there are no moving vans in a funeral cortege. Life itself, as "spirit," needs to be educated, corrected, encouraged, and consoled. We need others to counsel us, to forgive us, to put up with us, and to pray for us. The family is where these works of mercy are practiced in so normal and unpretentious a way that we don't even realize it. Yet once a family with small children loses its mother, everything begins to fall apart. The cruelest and most relentless form of poverty is that of street children, without parents and prey to the vultures.

We have asked for the grace to be signs and instruments. Now we have to "act," not only with gestures, but by projects and structures, by creating a culture of mercy. Once we begin, we sense immediately that the Spirit energizes and sustains these works. He does this by using the signs and instruments he wants, even if at times they do not appear to be the most suitable ones. It could even be said that, in order to carry out the works of mercy, the Spirit tends to choose the poorest, humblest, and most insignificant instruments, those who themselves most need that first ray of divine mercy. They are the ones who can best be shaped and readied to serve most effectively and well. The joy of realizing that we are "useless servants" whom the Lord blesses with the fruitfulness of his grace, seats at his table, and serves the Eucharist, is a confirmation that we are engaged in his works of mercy.

Our faithful people are happy to congregate around works of mercy. In penitential and festive celebrations, and in educational and charitable activities, our people willingly come together and let themselves be shepherded in ways that are not always recognized or appreciated, whereas so many of our more abstract and academic pastoral plans fail to work. The massive presence of our faithful people in our shrines and on our pilgrimages is an anonymous presence, but anonymous simply because it is made up of *so many* faces and so great a desire simply to be gazed upon with mercy by Jesus and Mary. The same can be said about the countless ways in which our people take part in countless initiatives of solidarity. This, too, needs to be recognized, appreciated, and promoted on our part.

As priests, we ask two graces of the Good Shepherd, that of letting ourselves be guided by the *sensus fidei* of our faithful people, and to be guided by their "sense of the poor." Both these "senses" have to do with the *sensus Christi,* with our people's love for, and faith in, Jesus.

Let us conclude by reciting the *Anima Christi,* that beautiful prayer that implores mercy from the Lord who came among us in the flesh and graciously feeds us with his body and blood. We ask him to show mercy to us and to his people. We ask his soul to "sanctify us," his body to "save us," his blood to "inebriate us" and to remove from us all other thirsts that are not of him. We ask the water flowing from his side "to wash us," his passion "to strengthen us." Comfort your people, crucified Lord! May your wounds "shelter us"....Grant that your people, Lord, may never be parted from you. Let nothing and no one separate us from your mercy, which defends us from the snares of the wicked enemy. Thus, we will sing your mercies, Lord, with all your saints when you bid us come to you.

PRAYER: ***Anima Christi***

Soul of Christ, sanctify me.
Body of Christ, save me.
Blood of Christ, inebriate me.
Water from the side of Christ, wash me.
Passion of Christ, strengthen me.
O Good Jesus, hear me.
Within the wounds, shelter me.
Permit me not to be separated from you.
From the wicked foe, defend me.
At the hour of my death, call me
And bid me come to You.
That with your saints I may praise You
Forever and ever.
Amen.

—Saint Ignatius of Loyola

Reflection Questions

1. *"Love for the poor has been the sign, the light that draws people to give glory to the Father. Our people value this in a priest who cares for the*

poor and the sick, for those whose sins he forgives and for those whom he patiently teaches and corrects."

What place does love for the poor have in your ministry? Which of the corporal and spiritual works of mercy have a prominent place in your priesthood, and how do they draw you closer to the Lord?

2. *"Being merciful is not only 'a way of life,' but 'the way of life.' There is no other way of being a priest."*

   In which ways does mercy live in your priesthood? How has this changed over time? In what ways would the people to whom you minister describe you as merciful?

3. Pope Francis spoke extensively about the priest in the sacrament of reconciliation. In what way do these phrases resonate with your experience as a confessor?

   - *"The confessor is not the master of God's forgiveness but its servant....*Signs and instruments *of an encounter. That is what we are."*
   - *"If people come to confession, it is because they are penitent;* repentance *is already present. They come to confession because they want to change."*
   - *"The rule of Jesus is to 'judge as we would be judged.' This is the key to our judgment: that we treat others with dignity, that we don't demean or mistreat them, that we help raise them up, and that we never forget that the Lord is using us, weak as we are, as his instruments."*
   - *"It is characteristic of mercy to cover sin with its cloak, so as not to wound people's dignity; like the two sons of Noah, who*

covered with a cloak the nakedness of their father in his drunkenness (cf. Gen 9:23)."

4. *"But if we look at the works of mercy as a whole, we see that the object of mercy is human life itself and everything it embraces. . . .Now we have to 'act,' not only with gestures, but by projects and structures, by creating a culture of mercy."*

   What difficulties do you encounter in creating a culture of mercy through your ministry? In what ways does creating a culture of mercy energize your priesthood? In what ways does mercy draw people to the life of the Church?

Homily for the Mass of the Sacred Heart of Jesus

This celebration of the Jubilee for Priests on the Solemnity of the Sacred Heart of Jesus invites us all to turn to the heart, the deepest root and foundation of every person, the focus of our affective life and, in a word, his or her very core. Today we contemplate two hearts: the *Heart of the Good Shepherd* and *our own heart as priests*.

The Heart of the Good Shepherd is not only the Heart that shows us mercy, but *is* itself mercy. There the Father's love shines forth; there I know I am welcomed and understood as I am; there, with all my sins and limitations, I know the certainty that I am chosen and loved. Contemplating that heart, I renew my first love: the memory of that time when the Lord touched my soul and called me to follow him, the memory of the joy of having cast the nets of our life upon the sea of his word (cf. Luke 5:5).

The Heart of the Good Shepherd tells us that his love is limitless; it is never exhausted and it never gives up. There we see his infinite and boundless self-giving; there we find the source of that faithful and meek love that sets free and makes others free; there we constantly discover anew that Jesus loves us "even to the end" (John 13:1)—it doesn't stop there, [but goes] even to the end—without ever being imposing.

The Heart of the Good Shepherd reaches out to us, above all to those who are most distant. There the needle of his compass inevitably points, there we see a particular "weakness" of his love, which desires to embrace all and lose none.

Contemplating the Heart of Christ, we are faced with the fundamental question of our priestly life: *Where is my heart directed?* (It's a question that we priests must ask ourselves many times, every day, every week: Where is my heart directed?) Our ministry is often full of plans, projects, and activities: from catechesis to liturgy, to works of charity, to pastoral and administrative commitments. Amid all these, we must still ask ourselves: What is my heart set on? Where is it directed? (What comes to mind is the beautiful prayer of the Liturgy, *Ubi vera Sunt Gaudia.*) What is the treasure that it seeks? For as Jesus says, "Where your treasure is, there will your heart be also" (Matt 6:21). (There are weaknesses in all of us, even sins. But let's go deeper, to the roots: Where is the root of our weaknesses, our sins, that is to say, what precisely is that "treasure" that distances us from the Lord?)

The great riches of the Heart of Jesus are two: the Father and ourselves. His days were divided between prayer to the Father and encountering people. (Not the distance, the encounter.) So, too, the heart of Christ's priests knows only two directions: *the Lord and his people.* The heart of the priest is a heart pierced by the love of the Lord. For this reason, he no longer looks to himself (he should not look at himself), but is turned toward God and his brothers and sisters. It is no longer "a fluttering heart," allured by momentary whims, shunning disagreements, and seeking petty satisfactions. Rather, it is a heart rooted firmly in the Lord, warmed by the Holy Spirit, open and available to our brothers and sisters. (And there, he resolves his sins.)

To help our hearts burn with the charity of Jesus the Good Shepherd, we can train ourselves to do three things suggested to us by today's readings: *seek out, include,* and *rejoice.*

Seek out. The prophet Ezekiel reminds us that God himself goes out in search of his sheep (Ezek 34:11, 16). As the Gospel says, he "goes out in search of the one who is lost" (Luke 15:4), without fear of the risks. Without delaying, he leaves the pasture and his regular workday. (And he does not make him pay 'overtime.') He does not put off the search. He does not think, "I have done enough for today; I'll worry about it tomorrow." Instead, he immediately sets to it; his heart is anxious until he finds that one lost sheep. Having found it, he forgets his weariness and puts the sheep on his shoulders, fully content. (Sometimes, he has to go out looking, talking, persuading; other times, he may have to remain before the tabernacle, wrestling with the Lord for that sheep.) That's the heart that seeks. It is a heart that does not privatize the times and spaces. Woe to the shepherds who privatize their ministry! Such is a heart that seeks out—a heart that does not set aside times and spaces as private, a heart that is not jealous of its legitimate quiet time and never demands that it be left alone. A shepherd after the heart of God does not protect his own comfort zone; he is not worried about protecting his good name, but rather, without fearing criticism, he is disposed to take risks in seeking to imitate his Lord. (Blessed are you when they insult you and persecute you and utter every kind of evil against you [falsely] because of me [Matt 5:11].)

A shepherd after the heart of God has a heart sufficiently free to set aside his own concerns. He does not live by calculating his gains or how long he has worked: he is not an accountant of the Spirit, but a Good Samaritan who seeks out those in need. For the flock he is a shepherd, not an inspector, and he devotes himself to the mission not 50 or 60 percent, but with all he has. In seeking, he finds, and he finds because he takes risks. He does not stop when disappointed, and he does not yield to weariness. Indeed, he is *stubborn in doing good,* anointed with the divine obstinacy that loses sight of no one. Not only does he keep his doors open, but he also goes to seek out those who no longer wish to enter them. Like every good Christian, and as an example for every Christian, he constantly *goes out of himself.* The epicenter of his heart is outside of himself. (It is decentralized from himself, but only in Jesus.) He is not drawn by his own "I," but by the "Thou" of God and by the "we" of other men and women.

Include. Christ loves and knows his sheep. He gives his life for them, and no one is a stranger to him (cf. John 10:11–14). His flock is his family and his life. He is not a boss to be feared by his flock, but a shepherd who walks alongside them and calls them by name (cf. John 10:3–4). He wants to gather the sheep that are not yet of his fold (cf. John 10:16). So it is also with the priest of Christ. He is anointed for his people, not to choose his own projects but to be close to the real men and women whom God has entrusted to him. No one is excluded from his heart, his prayers, or his smile. With a father's loving gaze and heart, he welcomes and includes everyone, and if at times he has to correct, it is to draw people closer. He stands apart from no one, but is always ready to dirty his hands. (The Good Shepherd doesn't know "gloves.") As a minister of the communion that he celebrates and lives, he does not await greetings and compliments from others, but is the first to reach out, rejecting gossip, judgments, and malice. He listens patiently to the problems of his people and accompanies them, sowing God's forgiveness with generous compassion. He does not scold those who wander off or lose their way, but is always ready to bring them back and to resolve difficulties and disagreements.

Rejoice. God is "full of joy" (cf. Luke 15:5). His joy is born of forgiveness, of life risen and renewed, of prodigal children who breathe once more the sweet air of home. The joy of Jesus the Good Shepherd is not a joy *for himself* alone, but a joy *for others and with others,* the true joy of love. This is also the joy of the priest. He is changed by the mercy that he *freely* gives. In prayer he discovers God's consolation and realizes that nothing is more powerful than his love. He thus experiences inner peace and is happy to be a channel of mercy, to bring men and women closer to the Heart of God. Sadness for him is not the norm, but only a step along the way; harshness is foreign to him, because he is a shepherd after the meek Heart of God.

Dear priests, in the Eucharistic celebration, we rediscover each day our identity as shepherds. In every Mass, may we truly make our own the words of Christ: "This is my body, which is given up for you." This is the meaning of our life; with these words, in a real way we can daily renew the promises we made at our priestly ordination. I thank all of you for saying yes (for so many hidden yeses everyday, that only the Lord knows). I thank you all for your yes *in giving your life in union with Jesus.* For in this is found the pure source of our joy.

Prayer on the Sacred Heart

O Infinite God
Make my heart like that of Your Son.
Make it as great and rich in love as His,
so that my brothers—or at least one of them,
sometime in my life—
can enter through this door
and there learn that You love him.
God of Our Lord Jesus Christ, let me find You in His Heart.
Amen.

—Karl Rahner, SJ

Reflection Questions

1. Pope Francis invites priests to see themselves in the Sacred Heart of Jesus, accepting this invitation to spend a moment of prayer with the following thoughts:

    - In the Heart of the Good Shepherd, *"the Father's love shines forth;*
    - *there I know I am welcomed and understood as I am;*

- *there, with all my sins and limitations, I know the certainty that I am chosen and loved.*
- *Contemplating that heart, I renew my first love: the memory of that time when the Lord touched my soul and called me to follow him,*
- *the memory of the joy of having cast the nets of our life upon the sea of his word (cf. Luke 5:5)."*

2. *"To help our hearts burn with the charity of Jesus the Good Shepherd, we can train ourselves to do three things suggested to us by today's readings:* seek out, include, *and* rejoice."

    How are these dimensions of priesthood present in your ministry? Which do you most enjoy, and which are the most difficult?

3. *"In every Mass, may we truly make our own the words of Christ: 'This is my body, which is given up for you.' This is the meaning of our life; with these words, in a real way we can daily renew the promises we made at our priestly ordination."*

    What is your experience of praying the words of institution? How do you experience the Body of Christ given up for you?

    What is this mystery like for you, joining your life to his, breaking open your life in priestly service of the people of God?